Sam Houston

A Fearless Statesman

Joanne Mattern

Consultant

Julie Hyman, MS.Ed.
Social Studies Coordinator
Birdville ISD

Publishing Credits

Dona Herweck Rice, *Editor-in-Chief*
Lee Aucoin, *Creative Director*
Marcus McArthur, Ph.D., *Associate Education Editor*
Neri Garcia, *Senior Designer*
Stephanie Reid, *Photo Editor*
Rachelle Cracchiolo, M.S.Ed., *Publisher*

Image Credits:

Cover North Wind Picture Archives and The State Preservation Board, Austin, Texas; p.1 North Wind Picture Archives; pp.2–3 State Preservation Board, Austin, Texas; p.4 LOC [LC–USZ62–27732]; pp.4–5 State Preservation Board, Austin, Texas.; p.6 Bridgeman Art Library; pp.6–7 The Granger Collection; p.7 (sidebar) The Granger Collection; p.8 Alamy; p.9 Bridgeman Art Library; p.10 North Wind Picture Archives; p.11 Tennessee State Library and Archives; p.11 (sidebar) North Wind Picture Archives; p.12 The Granger Collection; p.13 George Catlin (1834) [Public Domain]; p.14 North Wind Picture Archives; p.15 Corbis; p.15 (sidebar) LOC [LC–USZC4-6466]; p.16 (top) Sam Houston Memorial Museum; p.16 (bottom) Bridgeman Art Library; p.17 Cecily McNeil; p.17 (sidebar) LOC [LC-USZ62–53017]; p.18 The Granger Collection; p.19 North Wind Picture Archives; p.20 DeGolyer Library; p.21 (bottom) Houston Public Library; p.22 (top & bottom right) State Preservation Board, Austin, Texas; p.22 (bottom left) Bridgeman Art Library; p.23 Bridgeman Art Library; p.24 Alamy; p.25 North Wind Picture Archives; p.25 (sidebar) The Granger Collection; p.26 North Wind Picture Archives; p.27 The Granger Collection; p.27 (sidebar) Archive.org; pp.28–29 North Wind Picture Archives; p.29 (sidebar) J. Williams/Wikimedia; p.32 Alamy; All other images Shutterstock.

Teacher Created Materials
5301 Oceanus Drive
Huntington Beach, CA 92649-1030
http://www.tcmpub.com

ISBN 978-1-4333-5049-8

Printed by: 584728 Printed In: India PO#:16147

Table of Contents

A Texas Hero

Sam Houston is one of the greatest heroes in Texas history. Houston was the president of the **republic** of Texas. He was a United States **senator** and the governor of two states.

On March 2, 1836, Texas declared its independence, or freedom, from Mexico. But Mexico did not want to lose Texas. So Texas and Mexico went to war. Houston led the Texas Army. His courage and leadership helped Texas become an independent republic.

Sam Houston

As president of Texas, Houston tried to make peace with the American Indians. He also tried to pay off all of Texas's debts. He knew that Texas was not strong enough to stay its own country. So he pushed for Texas to become part of the United States.

Houston led Texas during an important time in Texas history. Today, the largest city in Texas **bears** his name.

the Battle of San Jacinto

Tall Texan

Military records state that Houston was 6 feet and 2 inches tall when he was 19 years old. However, legend says that Sam Houston was 6 feet and 6 inches (2 m) tall when he died. Either way, Houston was one tall Texan!

It's Everywhere!

Most cities in Texas have a Houston Street. There are also schools, parks, and museums named after Sam Houston. And, of course, there is the city of Houston, Texas. The city was named *Houston* following the Battle of San Jacinto (sahn ha-SEEN-toh).

Growing Up

The Young Houston

Sam Houston was born on March 2, 1793. He was born in Rockbridge County, Virginia. His parents were Samuel and Elizabeth Houston. Houston's father was a major-general in the U.S. Army. He also served in the local **militia** (mi-LISH-uh).

Samuel was away with the army most of the time, so Elizabeth ran the family farm by herself. She and her children worked hard, but they did not have much money.

Houston mostly went to school at home. He enjoyed reading and spending lots of time outdoors. He also loved **roaming** the woods and fields around the farm.

Sam Houston

In 1807, the Houstons decided to move west to Tennessee. Land was cheaper there, and the family wanted to make a new start. But Houston's father died before the family moved. His mother bought a farm and a general store. Houston worked on the farm and in the store, but he was bored. Soon, his life would be filled with adventures.

settlers moving west in the 1800s

Man the Militias!

Militias were an important part of life in the early days of the United States. The militia was a group of volunteers who trained to fight in times of emergency. In those days, the United States did not have a strong or large army. So local militias were needed to keep people safe.

A Hard Journey

Today, it is easy to travel between Virginia and Tennessee. But it was a hard trip in 1807. Houston and his family **endured** a long journey in a horse-drawn wagon. They faced poor roads, bad weather, accidents, and dangerous criminals.

Life with the Cherokee

Houston as an adopted Cherokee chief

Houston was starved for adventure. He also did not want to work on the farm or in the family store. So in 1809, he ran away from home and joined a local band of Cherokee (CHER-uh-kee) American Indians. The Cherokee welcomed Houston into the tribe. They liked Houston so much that their chief, Oolooteka (oo-loo-TAY-kuh), **adopted** Houston as his son. Oolooteka gave Houston the Cherokee name *Colonneh* (kuh-LAH-nee), which means "raven."

Houston lived with the Cherokee for three years. He dressed in Cherokee clothing, spoke their language, and adopted the customs of his tribe.

Trail of Tears

Finally, in 1812, Houston returned home because he owed people money and needed to pay off his **debts**. Houston opened a small school to earn money. He was able to pay back the money he owed quickly. Then, the War of 1812 started between the United States and Great Britain. Houston wanted to help defend his country. So he joined the U.S. Army.

The Cherokee

The Cherokee lived in the lands that are now the states of Georgia, Tennessee, North Carolina, South Carolina, Alabama, Kentucky, Virginia, and West Virginia. Over the years, they were forced to move from their homelands by the U.S. government. So many Cherokee died during the forced move in 1838 that the trip became known as the "Trail of Tears."

A Sign of Respect

The raven was a sacred, or **holy**, bird to the Cherokee. Naming Houston "the Raven" showed how much Chief Oolooteka respected Houston. Houston was proud to receive such an honor.

Serving His Country

The Battle of Horseshoe Bend

Houston joined the U.S. Army when he was 19 years old. Because his father had been an officer, Houston could have **enlisted** as an officer, too, but he wanted to earn his rank. So he joined the army as a **private**.

In 1814, Houston fought against a group of American Indians known as the Creek. The British had asked the Creek to fight against American settlers. The Creek had killed hundreds of settlers. Houston and American soldiers met the Creek in the Battle of Horseshoe Bend. Houston's officer was Andrew Jackson.

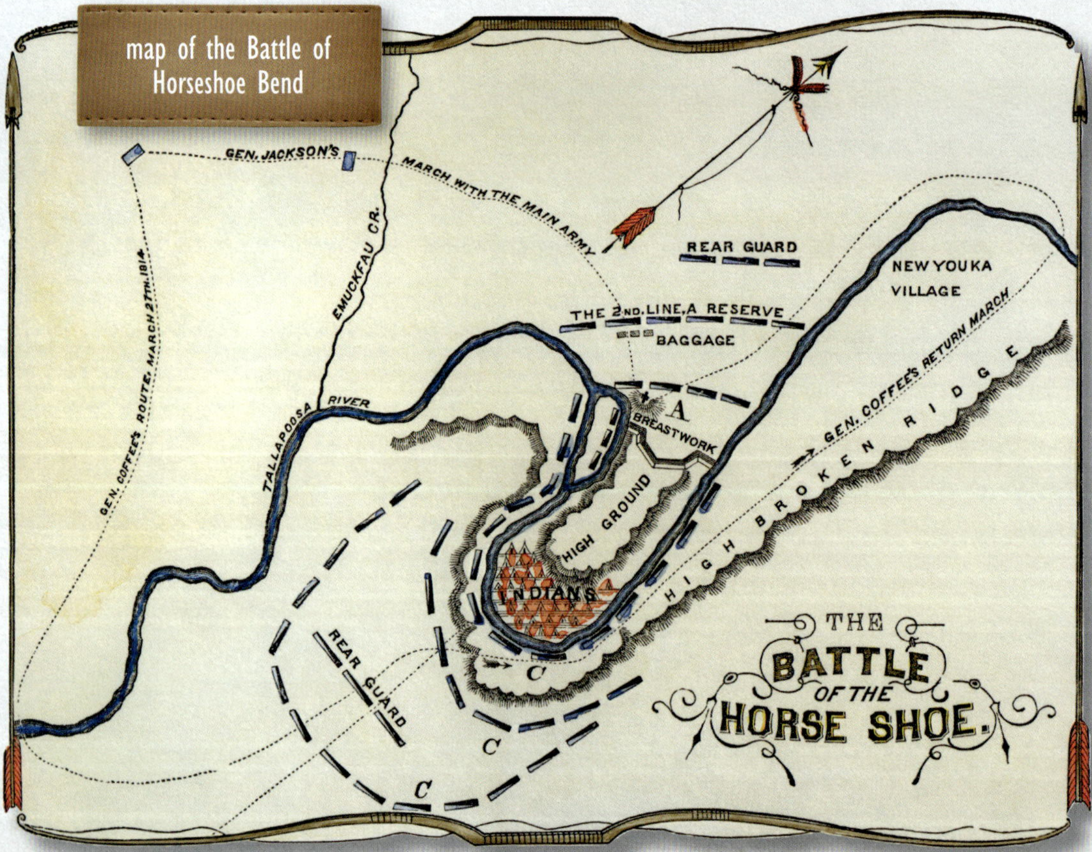

map of the Battle of Horseshoe Bend

Sam Houston during the Battle of Horseshoe Bend

During the battle, an arrow hit Houston in the leg. Jackson told Houston to leave the battle, but Houston refused. Instead, he led a charge against the Creek. During the charge, Houston was shot two more times. The United States won the battle, but Houston was badly hurt. Jackson was so impressed with Houston's bravery that he gave Houston a **promotion**. Houston was now an officer!

Serious Injuries

Houston was hurt badly at the Battle of Horseshoe Bend. Doctors even thought he would die. Though Houston survived, the injuries affected him for the rest of his life.

The War of 1812

The United States declared war on Great Britain in 1812. British ships had been stopping American ships, stealing their cargo, and even taking their sailors. The low point of the war for the Americans came in 1814, when the British invaded Washington, DC. They set the president's house on fire. But the Americans won the war in 1815.

naval battle in the War of 1812

An Unfair Treaty

In 1817, the U. S. government wanted to take away the Cherokee's land. The government wanted to give one million acres of its land to American settlers. In return, the United States would give the Cherokee money and land in Arkansas and Oklahoma. To do this, the government had to get the Cherokee to sign a **treaty**, or agreement.

Sam Houston with Chief Oolooteka

Chief Oolooteka

Andrew Jackson knew Houston was friendly with the Cherokee. The Cherokee trusted him. Jackson told Houston to talk Chief Oolooteka into signing the treaty. Houston did what he was told, even though he knew the treaty was unfair. He went to Washington, DC, to **protest** the agreement. While in Washington, DC, Houston was told he should not be wearing his Cherokee clothing in the **capital**. This greatly upset Houston. So he left the army.

Chief Oolooteka

Oolooteka was a Cherokee chief who lived in Tennessee. His English name was John Jolly. His Cherokee name, Oolooteka, means "He who puts away the drum." This name honored his skill as a peacemaker. There was no need for the war drum when Oolooteka was chief.

Indian Territory

Moving American Indians to Indian Territory was seen as a solution to the conflict between American Indians and American settlers who wanted the land. But the land given to the American Indians was not good land. It had bad soil and a dry climate that made farming very hard.

A New Life

In March 1818, Houston moved to Nashville, Tennessee to study law. The classes were supposed to take 18 months to complete. Houston finished the course in just six months! Houston was a very successful lawyer.

In 1820, Houston became a **colonel** in the Tennessee state military. Houston also got involved in politics. In 1823, Tennessee voters elected him to the U.S. House of Representatives. He represented his state in Washington, DC. Houston was now a **politician**.

Sam Houston, the politician

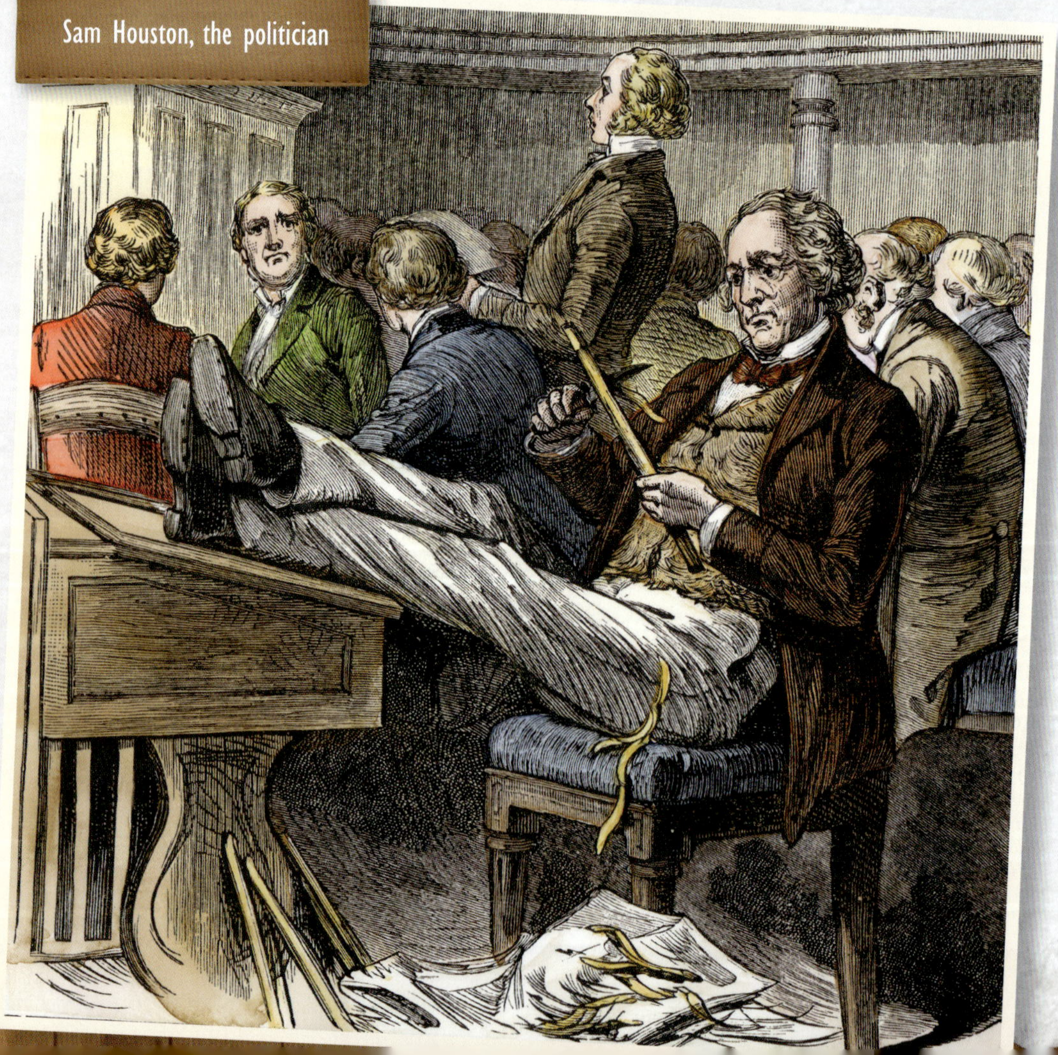

Houston no longer lived with the Cherokee. But he still liked to wear Cherokee clothes. He also wore fancy vests and shoes. Some people did not like Houston's style. They said he was showing off. But Houston was very popular.

In 1827, Houston became governor of Tennessee. During this time, his old friend Andrew Jackson was running for president. Governor Houston tried to talk people into voting for Jackson. In 1828, Jackson became the seventh president of the United States.

Old Hickory

Andrew Jackson was born in South Carolina in 1767. He entered politics after moving to Tennessee but became famous after being a hero during the War of 1812. He became president in 1828 and served until 1837. His nickname was "Old Hickory" because he was **stubborn** like hard hickory wood.

Law and Lawyers

Today, students must go to school for years and pass difficult tests to become lawyers. But during the 1800s, most lawyers learned the trade from other lawyers. They could even set up their own practice without any formal schooling.

Hard Times

In 1829, Houston married Eliza Allen. Houston was almost 36 years old, but Eliza was just a teenager. The marriage was very unhappy. After three months, Eliza left Houston and went back home.

Eliza Allen

Francis Scott Key is inspired during the War of 1812 and writes the national anthem.

Houston was embarrassed because many people believed that he had treated Eliza badly. He quit his job, left Tennessee, and returned to Chief Oolooteka and his Cherokee family.

The Cherokee accepted Houston again as a member of their tribe. Houston met a Cherokee woman named Tiana (tee-AH-nuh) Rogers. Soon, she and Houston fell in love.

In 1832, Houston went back to Washington, DC. A man named William Stanbery said Houston had cheated the Cherokee out of food from the government. Houston and Stanbery got into a fight. Stanbery tried to shoot Houston, and Houston beat Stanbery with his cane. Houston was arrested and fined for his actions. Many people thought he did the right thing. As a result, Houston became popular again.

William Stanbery

Francis Scott Key

A Famous Lawyer

After attacking Congressman Stanbery, Houston had to stand trial for his actions. Francis Scott Key represented Houston at his trial. Key was famous for writing the words to the U. S. national anthem, "The Star-Spangled Banner." Key wrote the anthem during the War of 1812.

Tiana Rogers

Houston probably met his Cherokee wife long before they fell in love. Houston became friends with Tiana's brothers back in 1809, when he first moved in with the Cherokee in Tennessee.

Trouble in Texas

Houston to the Rescue

In 1832, President Jackson sent Houston to Texas. At that time, Texas was part of Mexico. Many people from the United States had settled in Texas. But they did not like the rules Mexico had set for them. Jackson asked Houston to find out what was happening between the settlers and the Mexicans. Later, Jackson also asked Houston to make peace treaties with several American Indian tribes in Texas.

Houston's wife, Tiana, did not want to go to Texas with him, so Houston headed west by himself. He set up a law office in the town of Nacogdoches (nak-uh-DOH-chuhz). Houston soon became a popular and powerful figure in Texas.

the United States in the 1830s

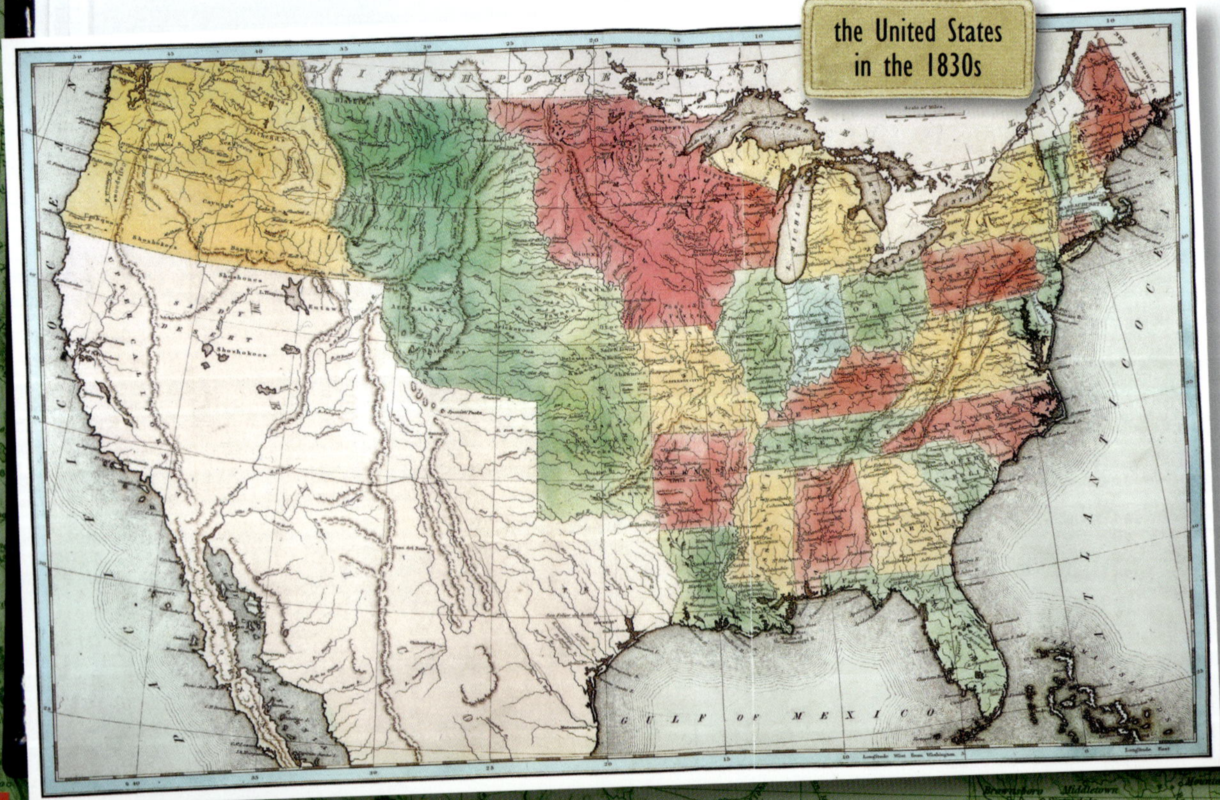

Santa Anna

It was clear to Houston that Texas and Mexico were going to fight. Mexican President Antonio López de Santa Anna (ahn-TOH-nee-oh LOH-pehs deh sahn-tah AH-nah) refused to listen to the Texans' demands. The Texans asked Houston to help them. In 1835, Houston helped set up a Texas government and became one of the military leaders. Texans wanted their independence.

Santa Anna

Santa Anna was born in Mexico in 1794. He went on to become one of the most powerful men in Mexican history. He became Mexico's top military leader and was elected president in 1833. He remained president until he was removed from office in 1855. He died in 1876.

From Spain to Mexico

At first, Mexico was ruled by Spain. Mexico won its freedom from Spain in 1821. At the time, Mexico included all of the modern-day American Southwest.

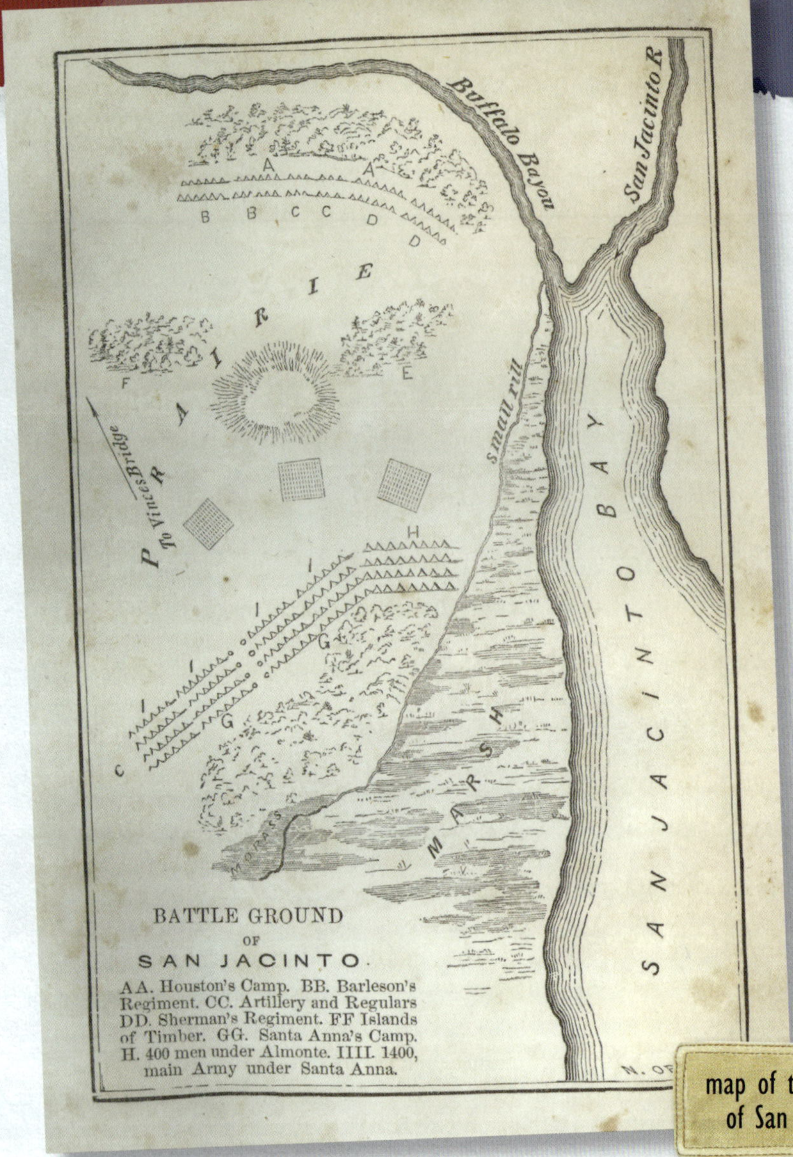

map of the Battle of San Jacinto

Declaring Independence

On March 2, 1836, Texas declared its independence from Mexico. Two days later, Houston was elected major-general of the Texas Army.

Fewer than 200 Texans gathered in a church called the *Alamo*. On March 6, Santa Anna led about 1,800 Mexican soldiers against the Alamo. Almost every Texan at the Alamo was killed.

Houston knew it would be hard for his small army to defeat Santa Anna. Houston headed east. Santa Anna followed. Many people **criticized** Houston for running away. But he had a plan.

On April 21, 1836, the two armies met at the San Jacinto River. Santa Anna was confident that his army could beat the Texans. So he let them take an afternoon nap. Houston attacked while the Mexican army slept. The Battle of San Jacinto was over in just 18 minutes. The Texans defeated the larger Mexican Army. They had won their freedom!

General Sam Houston

the Alamo today

The Alamo

The Alamo was a Spanish **mission** built in 1718. Today, it is a museum and one of the most popular sites in Texas. Thousands of people visit the Alamo every year. The site is called the "Shrine of Texas Liberty."

The Runaway Scrape

Houston's army was not the only thing moving east in 1836. Many Texas settlers also fled their homes to get away from the invading Mexican Army. They returned home after they learned that Houston had defeated Santa Anna at the Battle of San Jacinto. That journey to East Texas is called the *Runaway Scrape*.

Struggle for Statehood

Leading Texas

Texas was now a free republic. On September 5, 1836, Houston was elected president of Texas. He ran the government from a log house in Houston, a city that had been named after him. His vice president, Mirabeau Lamar, had also fought at the Battle of San Jacinto. However, he and Houston did not like each other. They had very different ideas about what was best for Texas.

President Sam Houston

Vice-President Mirabeau Lamar

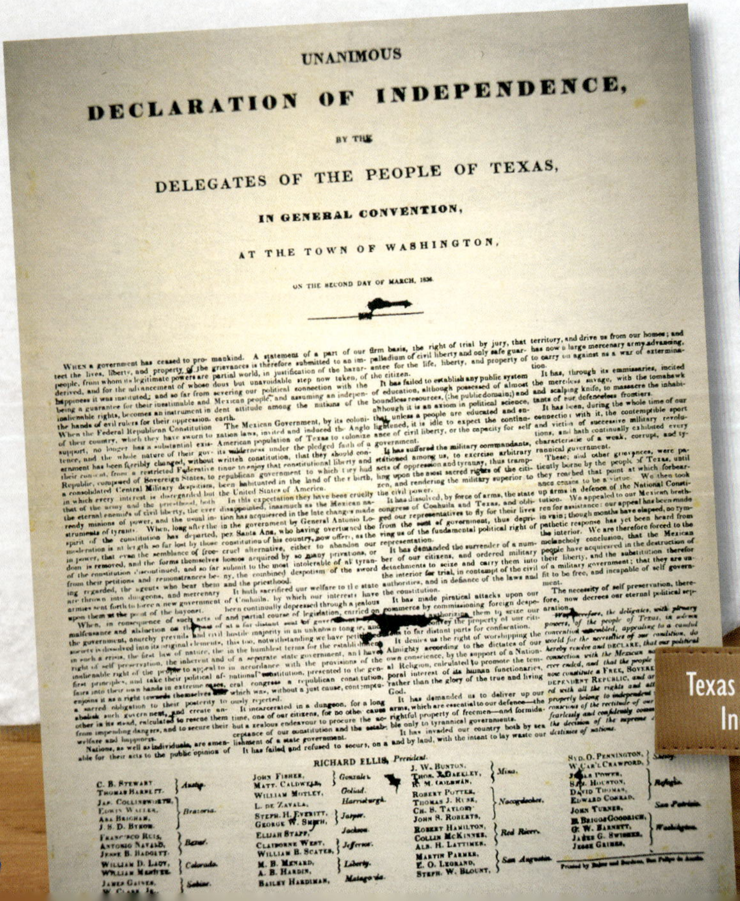

UNANIMOUS

DECLARATION OF INDEPENDENCE,

BY THE

DELEGATES OF THE PEOPLE OF TEXAS,

IN GENERAL CONVENTION,

AT THE TOWN OF WASHINGTON,

ON THE SECOND DAY OF MARCH, 1836.

Texas Declaration of Independence

Santa Anna attacks Texans after the war ended.

The war was over, but Houston faced many problems. The biggest problem was money. Houston had to find ways for Texas to repay its debts. He tried to be fair to the American Indians in Texas, too. He wanted to set aside land where they could live.

Santa Anna posed another problem for Houston. The Mexican president had signed a peace treaty after the war. He promised to leave Texas alone. But Santa Anna did not keep his word.

Troublemaker

Many people felt that Houston should have killed Santa Anna after the Battle of San Jacinto. Instead, he allowed Santa Anna to live after he signed a peace treaty with Texas. But Santa Anna did not do what he promised and was soon attacking Texas again.

Houston, Texas

In August 1836, two brothers founded Houston, Texas. They named the new city in honor of the hero of the Texas Revolution. They hoped Houston would become the capital of Texas. Instead, Austin was named the Texas capital in 1839.

Sam Houston

A Dream Come True

Houston's term as president ended in 1838. Texas law said he could not serve two terms **consecutively**, or in a row. Houston was replaced by his vice president, Mirabeau Lamar, who changed almost everything Houston had done. Lamar ran up debts and forced American Indians in Texas to move to Oklahoma.

Texas voters reelected Houston as president in 1841. He found ways for Texas to pay off the money it owed. He also kept talking to the United States about statehood. Houston knew that Texas was not strong enough to stay independent. Santa Anna wanted to make Texas part of Mexico again. Joining the United States was the best way for Texas to survive.

Texas faced several Mexican attacks during 1842. Houston knew that Texas could not hold off Mexico forever. He worked hard to convince Texans that they needed the United States' help.

This map shows the territory claimed by Texas when it was admitted to the U.S. in 1845.

Houston's term ended in 1843, but he kept working to make Texas a state. Finally, in 1845, Houston's wish came true. On December 29, Texas became the 28th state in the United States.

Margaret Lea

Lasting Love

Houston was visiting a friend in Alabama when he met 20-year-old Margaret Lea. The two fell in love and married on May 9, 1840. They went on to have eight children together. They remained married until Houston's death in 1863.

Mexican-American War

After Texas became part of the United States, the United States fought a war with Mexico to protect its new addition. The Mexican-American War lasted from 1846 until the United States won in 1848.

A Nation Divided

Texas was now a state. It had to elect senators to represent them in Washington, DC. Houston was one of the state's first senators. He served three terms in the U.S. Senate.

During the 1850s, slavery was **controversial** in the United States. Many people in the North thought that slavery was wrong. Many people in the South disagreed. They wanted slaves to work on their large cotton and tobacco **plantations**.

Slaves pick cotton on a plantation in the South.

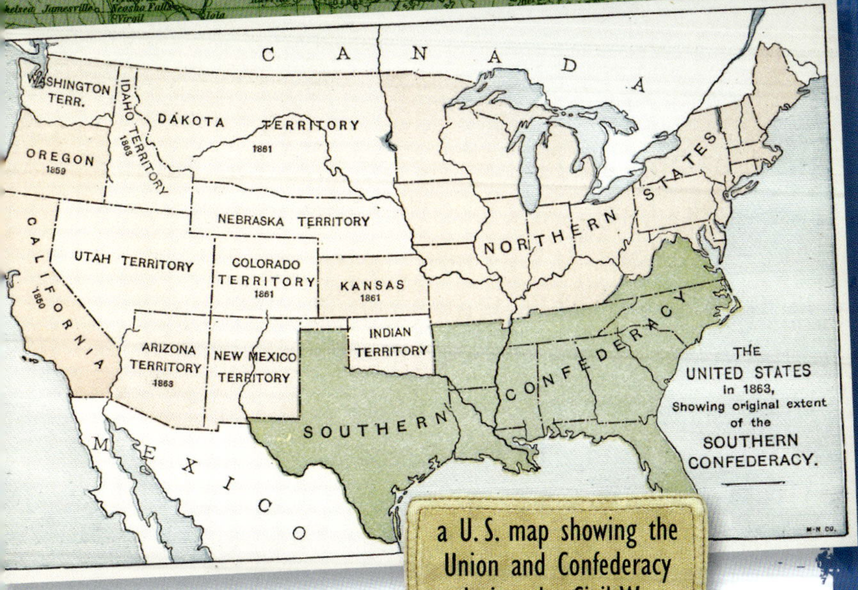

a U.S. map showing the Union and Confederacy during the Civil War

Many Southern states said they would **secede** (si-SEED) from, or leave, the United States if slavery were outlawed. They wanted to form their own country. This country would be called the *Confederate States of America*, or the ***Confederacy***. Many people in Texas wanted to secede, too. Houston thought this was a bad idea. In 1859, he decided to run for Texas governor again. He believed he could keep Texas in the Union.

Houston won the election. However, in 1861, the people of Texas voted to secede from the United States. Texas joined the Confederacy. But Houston refused to support the Confederacy. So he stepped down from his office.

Slavery Issues

Houston was not against slavery. In fact, he owned slaves. However, Houston did not want the nation to be torn apart by slavery. He felt there should be a peaceful solution that would allow people to keep slaves and still remain part of the United States.

The Confederacy

The Confederacy was made up of 11 Southern states that seceded from the Union in 1861. The Confederate president was Jefferson Davis. No foreign governments ever recognized the Confederacy.

Jefferson Davis

Final Days

After Houston **retired**, he and his family moved to Cedar Point on Galveston Bay. Two weeks later, the Civil War began, and Union gunboats filled Galveston's harbor. It was not safe to stay there any longer. In 1862, the Houstons moved to Huntsville, Texas. They moved into an unusual house that was shaped like a steamboat!

Houston's health began to fail. He caught many colds and lung infections. Finally, on July 26, 1863, Houston died of **pneumonia** (noo-MOHN-yuh). His last words were said to have been, "Texas… Texas…Margaret." Houston was 70 years old.

Houston was one of the most important men in Texas history. His strength and ideas helped win Texas freedom from Mexico. Later, Houston guided Texas to become an American state. He built a strong government. He tried to treat all of Texas's people fairly. Although he faced many challenges in his life, Houston always did what he thought was best for his beloved Texas.

the Battle of Galveston

A House Divided

The Civil War lasted from 1861 until 1865. At first, the South won most of the battles. But the North had more money and factories. It was able to produce more guns, ammunition, and supplies. By 1865, the South was in ruins and the war was over.

Houston's Burial Place

Sam Houston was buried in Huntsville, Texas. Ten years after his death, the simple marker on his grave was replaced by a 25-foot (8 m) piece of granite. The stone was engraved with a tribute from Andrew Jackson that read, "The world will take care of Houston's fame."

Houston's grave

Glossary

adopted—to take as one's own

bears—to have as a feature or a trait

capital—the location of a government

colonel—a high officer rank, just below general

Confederacy—the government of the Southern states that seceded from the United States between 1861 and 1865

consecutively—in a row; one after the other

controversial—relating to a difference of opinion or conflict

criticized—spoke badly about a person or his actions

debts—money owed to another person or people

endured—to bear or suffer patiently

enlisted—signed up for a branch of the armed forces

holy—respected as sacred

militia—a group of citizen soldiers

mission—religious and military outpost established by the Spanish during colonization

plantations—types of large farms found in the southern United States

pneumonia—a serious lung infection that makes it hard to breathe

politician—a person who runs for or holds public office

private—a low ranking for a soldier

promotion—a moving up in rank

protest—to object strongly

republic—a political system in which people elect representatives to make laws for them

retired—to have given up one's job

roaming—to go from place to place without a plan

secede—to leave a country and form a new government

senator—an elected member of the U.S. Senate

stubborn—hard to convince, persuade, or move

treaty—a legal agreement between two governments

Index

Your Turn!

Sam Houston craved adventure. As a young man, he found it by running away from home to live with the Cherokee American Indians. He learned the Cherokee language, wore traditional clothing, and was accepted as a member of the tribe. Later, Houston married a Cherokee woman.

Sincerely, Sam Houston

Write a letter to a friend from Sam Houston's point of view. Explain how his American Indian friends influenced his ideas about government.